PROVOKED INTO PURPOSE WORKBOOK

WRITTEN BY QU'DERRICK R. COVINGTON

WWW.QRCOVINGTON.COM

For more information, email info@qrcovington.com.

Walking in your purpose isn't about comfort; it's about growth. True fulfillment comes when you step beyond your fear and embrace the discomfort that pushes you forward.

Qu'Derrick R. Covington

I WANT TO HEAR FROM YOU!

Once you've completed the workbook I invite you to Scan the QR code to provide your input and help improve the Provoked Into Purpose.

Your feedback is invaluable!

WWW.QRCOVINGTON.COM

Dear Reader,

Welcome to the Provoked Into Purpose Workbook. This journey you are about to embark on is one that will guide you in uncovering your passions, aligning them with your purpose, and taking actionable steps toward living a fulfilled life. If you're holding this workbook, it's because you are ready to go beyond simply reading about purpose—you're ready to dive deep, reflect, and take action.

Each section in this workbook is designed to complement the lessons and reflections from Provoked Into Purpose. You will find questions that challenge you, activities that provoke you, and exercises that will help you move from thought to action. The goal is for you to not only gain clarity but to fully commit to the process of walking into the life you were created to live.

Remember, the work of self-discovery and growth isn't always easy, but it's necessary for unlocking the full potential that lies within you. Use this workbook as your guide, and come back to it often. Each time you engage with the material, you will uncover new insights about yourself and your purpose.

Let this be your personal companion as you embark on this exciting journey to living a life of passion, purpose, and meaning.

With gratitude and encouragement,
Qu'Derrick R. Covington

SECTION ONE

Now that you've reflected on the significance of your beginnings, it's time to explore how your past can propel you toward your purpose.

BEYOND BEGINNINGS

WWW.QRCOVINGTON.COM

Write down three key experiences and reflect on how they influence your life currently.

- What challenges or circumstances from your early life have shaped who you are today?
- How have these experiences provoked you into seeking something greater?
- What lessons have you learned from your past that you can apply to your purpose-driven life?

1

2

3

Letter to Your Younger Self:
Write a letter to your younger self. Offer advice, encouragement, and lessons you've learned from your journey so far.

TAKE YOUR JOURNEY TO THE NEXT LEVEL

You've made incredible progress through this section, but your journey toward living fully in your purpose is just beginning. If you're ready to dive deeper, work directly with me, Qu'Derrick R. Covington, as your personal purpose coach. Together, we will continue to uncover your passions, develop a roadmap to success, and ensure you have the mindset and tools needed to live out your purpose.

Scan the QR Code below to schedule a 1-on-1 session or to learn more about my speaking engagements and coaching programs.

testimonials

Marquis Thorpe
Chief of Staff, National Security at AWS

QuDerrick Covington's visionary leadership is evident in his ability to conceptualize and implement innovative strategies that propel teams towards their goals, showcasing a keen foresight for the organization's future.

Dr. Roderick Heath
Asst. Vice Chancellor & Dean of Students at Fayetteville State University

As a leader, QuDerrick Covington's vision and strategic thinking have guided teams to unprecedented success, earning him the reputation of an outstanding and influential figure in the industry.

Dr. Tyson Beale
Vice President Student Affairs at Prince George's Community College

QuDerrick Covington's public speaking is unmatched, creating an engaging and inclusive atmosphere at every event. His charisma and seamless execution make him a standout speaker, leaving a lasting positive impact on every attendee.

You can't be competitive without knowing your purpose.

HEAD OVER TO INSTAGRAM & FOLLOW **@QRCOVINGTON** FOR DAILY INSPIRATION + PURPOSE-DRIVEN INSIGHTS!

SECTION TWO

Passion is the fuel for your purpose.
Take a moment to list your top five passions and discover how they are already showing up in your life.

THE PASSION PATHWAY

WWW.QRCOVINGTON.COM

Discover your passions and understand how they signal your true purpose.

1 What activities or topics make you feel most alive and energized?

2 What are the things you would do even if you weren't being paid?

3 How can these passions be integrated into your daily life?

LIST YOUR TOP FIVE PASSIONS.

For each passion, write down one actionable step you can take this week to pursue it further.

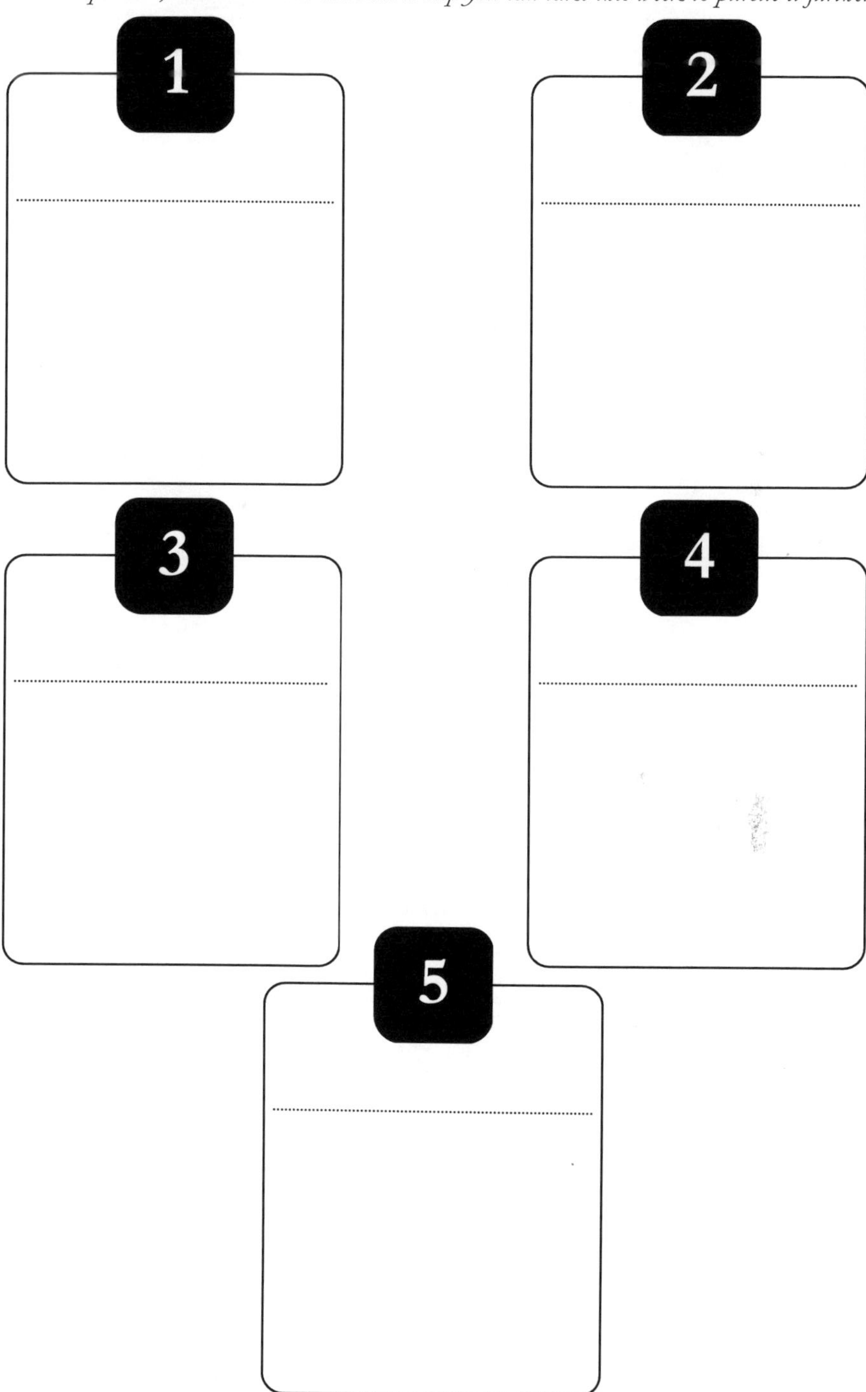

TAKE YOUR JOURNEY TO THE NEXT LEVEL

You've made incredible progress through this section, but your journey toward living fully in your purpose is just beginning. If you're ready to dive deeper, work directly with me, Qu'Derrick R. Covington, as your personal purpose coach. Together, we will continue to uncover your passions, develop a roadmap to success, and ensure you have the mindset and tools needed to live out your purpose.

Scan the QR Code below to schedule a 1-on-1 session or to learn more about my speaking engagements and coaching programs.

testimonials

Marquis Thorpe
Chief of Staff, National Security at AWS

QuDerrick Covington's visionary leadership is evident in his ability to conceptualize and implement innovative strategies that propel teams towards their goals, showcasing a keen foresight for the organization's future.

Dr. Roderick Heath
Asst. Vice Chancellor & Dean of Students at Fayetteville State University

As a leader, QuDerrick Covington's vision and strategic thinking have guided teams to unprecedented success, earning him the reputation of an outstanding and influential figure in the industry.

Dr. Tyson Beale
Vice President Student Affairs at Prince George's Community College

QuDerrick Covington's public speaking is unmatched, creating an engaging and inclusive atmosphere at every event. His charisma and seamless execution make him a standout speaker, leaving a lasting positive impact on every attendee.

You can't be competitive without knowing your purpose.

HEAD OVER TO INSTAGRAM & FOLLOW **@QRCOVINGTON** FOR DAILY INSPIRATION + PURPOSE-DRIVEN INSIGHTS!

SECTION THREE

Our connections shape our journey.
Who are the people who
inspire and support your purpose?

PURPOSED CONNECTIONS

WWW.QRCOVINGTON.COM

LIST FIVE PEOPLE WHO CURRENTLY SUPPORT OR INSPIRE YOU.

Identify and cultivate relationships that support your purpose.

1 List five names of who currently support or inspire you.

- Write a name in each circle. In the same circle of each name write how they contribute to your growth and purpose?

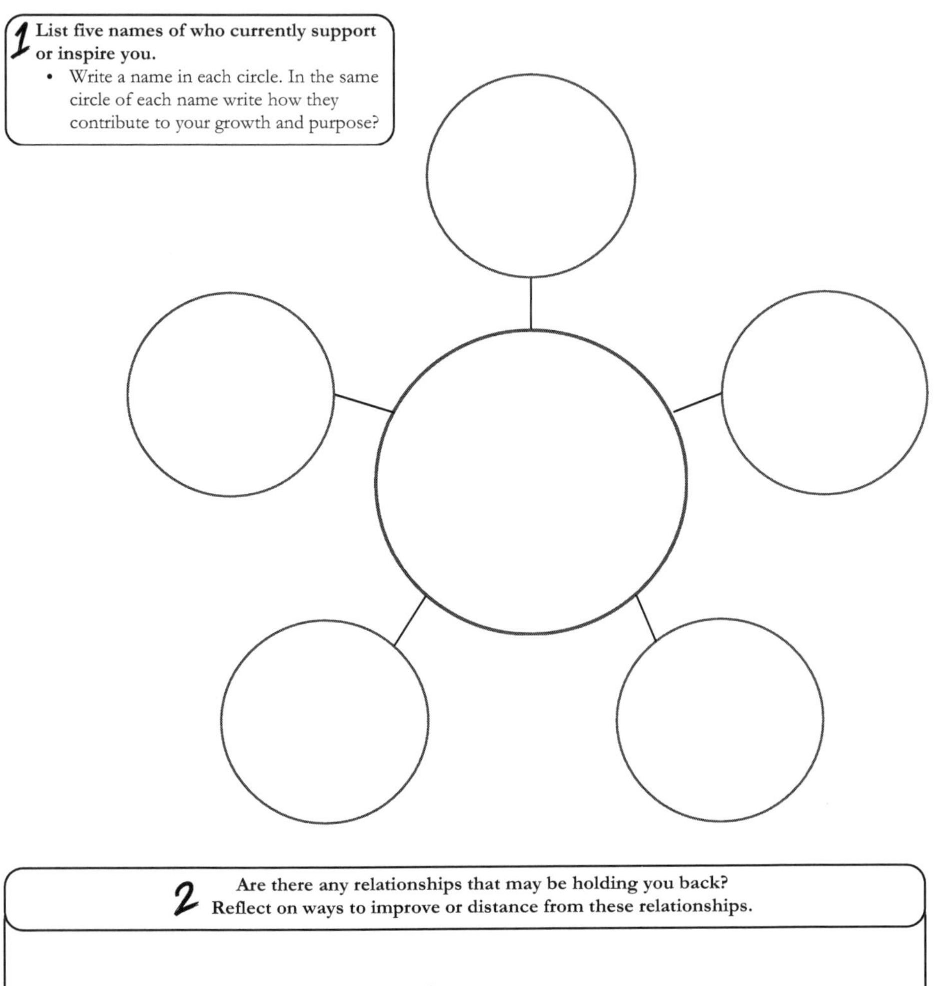

2 Are there any relationships that may be holding you back? Reflect on ways to improve or distance from these relationships.

3

Reach out to one person in your network this week.
Schedule a meeting or conversation to discuss your goals and ask for guidance or mentorship.

Notes:

TAKE YOUR JOURNEY TO THE NEXT LEVEL

You've made incredible progress through this section, but your journey toward living fully in your purpose is just beginning. If you're ready to dive deeper, work directly with me, Qu'Derrick R. Covington, as your personal purpose coach. Together, we will continue to uncover your passions, develop a roadmap to success, and ensure you have the mindset and tools needed to live out your purpose.

Scan the QR Code below to schedule a 1-on-1 session or to learn more about my speaking engagements and coaching programs.

testimonials

Marquis Thorpe

Chief of Staff, National Security at AWS

QuDerrick Covington's visionary leadership is evident in his ability to conceptualize and implement innovative strategies that propel teams towards their goals, showcasing a keen foresight for the organization's future.

Dr. Roderick Heath

Asst. Vice Chancellor & Dean of Students at Fayetteville State University

As a leader, QuDerrick Covington's vision and strategic thinking have guided teams to unprecedented success, earning him the reputation of an outstanding and influential figure in the industry.

Dr. Tyson Beale

Vice President Student Affairs at Prince George's Community College

QuDerrick Covington's public speaking is unmatched, creating an engaging and inclusive atmosphere at every event. His charisma and seamless execution make him a standout speaker, leaving a lasting positive impact on every attendee.

You can't be competitive without knowing your purpose.

HEAD OVER TO INSTAGRAM & FOLLOW **@QRCOVINGTON** FOR DAILY INSPIRATION + PURPOSE-DRIVEN INSIGHTS!

SECTION FOUR

Growth often comes from discomfort. What areas in your life are pushing you to evolve?

PURPOSED DISCOMFORT

WWW.QRCOVINGTON.COM

EMBRACE DISCOMFORT AS A CATALYST FOR GROWTH

Part 1: Identifying Discomfort

Write down one area of your life where you feel discomfort (career, relationships, personal growth, etc.). How does this discomfort relate to your purpose? How is it pushing you to grow?

EMBRACE DISCOMFORT AS A CATALYST FOR GROWTH
Part 2: Confronting Fear

Identify one fear that has been holding you back.
What steps can you take this week to confront or challenge that fear? Write down your plan.

TAKE YOUR JOURNEY TO THE NEXT LEVEL

You've made incredible progress through this section, but your journey toward living fully in your purpose is just beginning. If you're ready to dive deeper, work directly with me, Qu'Derrick R. Covington, as your personal purpose coach. Together, we will continue to uncover your passions, develop a roadmap to success, and ensure you have the mindset and tools needed to live out your purpose.

Scan the QR Code below to schedule a 1-on-1 session or to learn more about my speaking engagements and coaching programs.

testimonials

Marquis Thorpe
Chief of Staff, National Security at AWS

QuDerrick Covington's visionary leadership is evident in his ability to conceptualize and implement innovative strategies that propel teams towards their goals, showcasing a keen foresight for the organization's future.

Dr. Roderick Heath
Asst. Vice Chancellor & Dean of Students at Fayetteville State University

As a leader, QuDerrick Covington's vision and strategic thinking have guided teams to unprecedented success, earning him the reputation of an outstanding and influential figure in the industry.

Dr. Tyson Beale
Vice President Student Affairs at Prince George's Community College

QuDerrick Covington's public speaking is unmatched, creating an engaging and inclusive atmosphere at every event. His charisma and seamless execution make him a standout speaker, leaving a lasting positive impact on every attendee.

You can't be competitive without knowing your purpose.

HEAD OVER TO INSTAGRAM & FOLLOW **@QRCOVINGTON**
FOR DAILY INSPIRATION + PURPOSE-DRIVEN INSIGHTS!

SECTION FIVE

To walk in your purpose, you need to eliminate distractions and stay focused on your path.

SHIFTING THE NOISE

WWW.QRCOVINGTON.COM

LEARN TO FILTER OUT NEGATIVITY AND STAY FOCUSED ON YOUR PATH.
Part 1: Eliminating Distractions

List three distractions (people, activities, habits) that are currently taking you off your path.
What strategies can you use to minimize or eliminate these distractions?

Distraction 1

Strategy

01
02
03
04
05

Distraction 2

Strategy

01
02
03
04
05

Distraction 3

Strategy

01
02
03
04
05

1. What voices or opinions have been distracting you from your purpose?
2. How can you create boundaries to protect your mental and emotional well-being?
3. What are your internal sources of negativity, and how can you address them?

LEARN TO FILTER OUT NEGATIVITY AND STAY FOCUSED ON YOUR PATH.

Part 2: Daily Affirmation

Write a daily affirmation that reminds you of your purpose and keeps you focused.
Feel free to write more than one affirmation. I've added one to help you get started.
Recite this affirmation every morning for the next week.

I am walking boldly in my purpose, embracing every challenge as an opportunity for growth, and trusting that my passions will guide me to the life I am destined to live.

TAKE YOUR JOURNEY TO THE NEXT LEVEL

You've made incredible progress through this section, but your journey toward living fully in your purpose is just beginning. If you're ready to dive deeper, work directly with me, Qu'Derrick R. Covington, as your personal purpose coach. Together, we will continue to uncover your passions, develop a roadmap to success, and ensure you have the mindset and tools needed to live out your purpose.

Scan the QR Code below to schedule a 1-on-1 session or to learn more about my speaking engagements and coaching programs.

testimonials

Marquis Thorpe
Chief of Staff, National Security at AWS

QuDerrick Covington's visionary leadership is evident in his ability to conceptualize and implement innovative strategies that propel teams towards their goals, showcasing a keen foresight for the organization's future.

Dr. Roderick Heath
Asst. Vice Chancellor & Dean of Students at Fayetteville State University

As a leader, QuDerrick Covington's vision and strategic thinking have guided teams to unprecedented success, earning him the reputation of an outstanding and influential figure in the industry.

Dr. Tyson Beale
Vice President Student Affairs at Prince George's Community College

QuDerrick Covington's public speaking is unmatched, creating an engaging and inclusive atmosphere at every event. His charisma and seamless execution make him a standout speaker, leaving a lasting positive impact on every attendee.

You can't be competitive without knowing your purpose.

HEAD OVER TO INSTAGRAM & FOLLOW **@QRCOVINGTON**
FOR DAILY INSPIRATION + PURPOSE-DRIVEN INSIGHTS!

SECTION SIX

Living a life of purpose doesn't mean sacrificing prosperity.

PURPOSE WITH PROSPERITY

WWW.QRCOVINGTON.COM

ALIGN YOUR FINANCIAL GOALS WITH YOUR PURPOSE.

Financial Goal Setting

How do these goals align with your purpose?

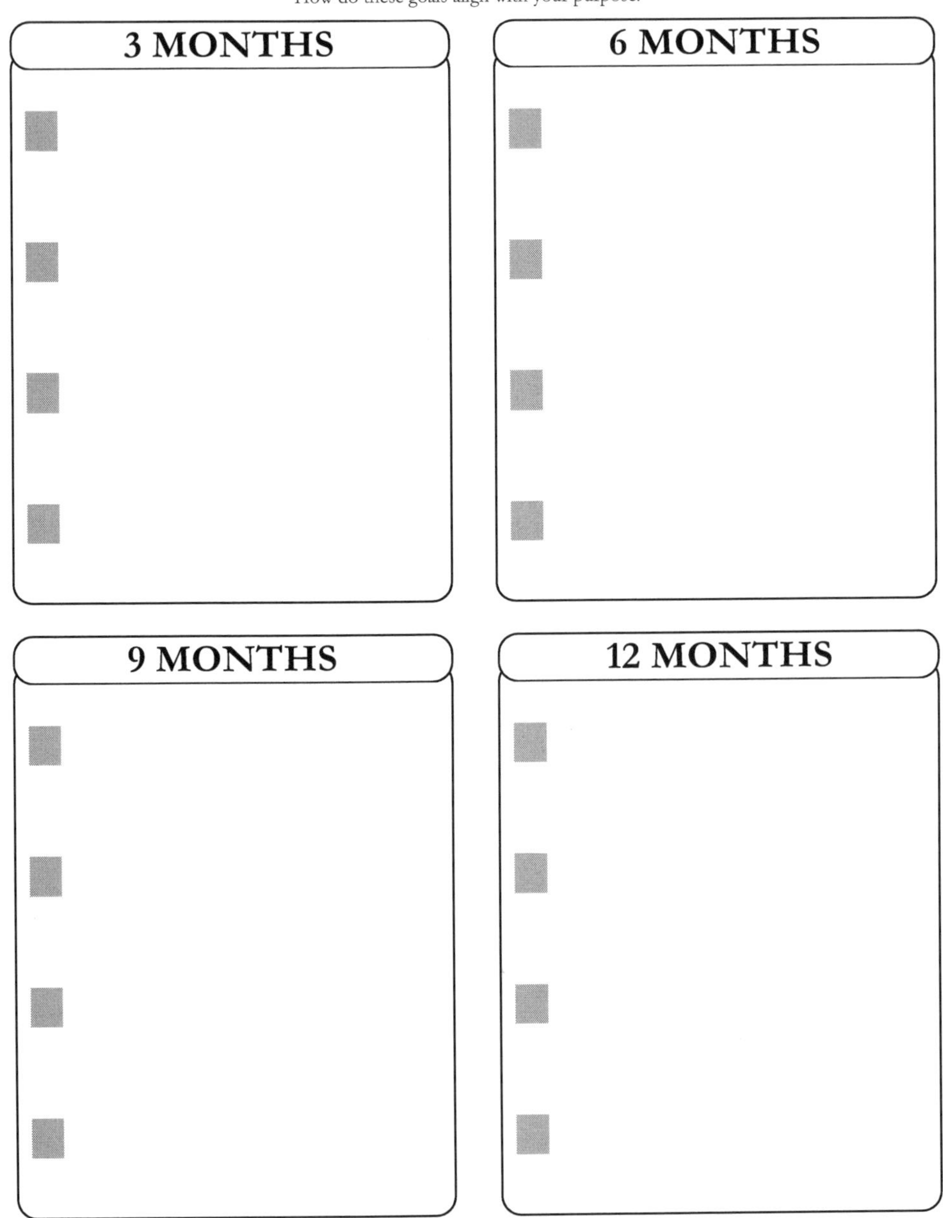

Write down three ways you can invest in yourself or your purpose over the next year.

1. ....
2. ....
3. ....

ALIGN YOUR FINANCIAL GOALS WITH YOUR PURPOSE.

Financial Goal Setting

How do your financial goals align with your purpose?

1. How can you balance the pursuit of financial success with living a purpose-driven life?
2. What financial goals support your purpose, and how can you achieve them?
3. How does your current definition of prosperity align with your values?

TAKE YOUR JOURNEY TO THE NEXT LEVEL

You've made incredible progress through this section, but your journey toward living fully in your purpose is just beginning. If you're ready to dive deeper, work directly with me, Qu'Derrick R. Covington, as your personal purpose coach. Together, we will continue to uncover your passions, develop a roadmap to success, and ensure you have the mindset and tools needed to live out your purpose.

Scan the QR Code below to schedule a 1-on-1 session or to learn more about my speaking engagements and coaching programs.

testimonials

Marquis Thorpe
Chief of Staff, National Security at AWS

QuDerrick Covington's visionary leadership is evident in his ability to conceptualize and implement innovative strategies that propel teams towards their goals, showcasing a keen foresight for the organization's future.

Dr. Roderick Heath
Asst. Vice Chancellor & Dean of Students at Fayetteville State University

As a leader, QuDerrick Covington's vision and strategic thinking have guided teams to unprecedented success, earning him the reputation of an outstanding and influential figure in the industry.

Dr. Tyson Beale
Vice President Student Affairs at Prince George's Community College

QuDerrick Covington's public speaking is unmatched, creating an engaging and inclusive atmosphere at every event. His charisma and seamless execution make him a standout speaker, leaving a lasting positive impact on every attendee.

You can't be competitive without knowing your purpose.

HEAD OVER TO INSTAGRAM & FOLLOW **@QRCOVINGTON** FOR DAILY INSPIRATION + PURPOSE-DRIVEN INSIGHTS!

SECTION SEVEN

Strengthen your conviction and build a winning mindset by reflecting on your core beliefs.

CONVICTION & WINNING BELIEFS

WWW.QRCOVINGTON.COM

STRENGTHEN YOUR CONVICTION AND ADOPT A WINNING MINDSET.

Part 1: Identify Your Core Convictions

1 What are the core beliefs that drive your purpose?
Write down three core convictions that guide your actions and decisions.

My Core Beliefs	1
2	3

2 Write about a time when you overcame doubt or fear to achieve success.
How can you apply that winning mindset to your current challenges?

....

....

....

....

....

....

....

STRENGTHEN YOUR CONVICTION AND ADOPT A WINNING MINDSET.

Part 2: Owning a Winning Mindset

Write a personal mission statement that reflects your conviction and winning mindset.

TAKE YOUR JOURNEY TO THE NEXT LEVEL

You've made incredible progress through this section, but your journey toward living fully in your purpose is just beginning. If you're ready to dive deeper, work directly with me, Qu'Derrick R. Covington, as your personal purpose coach. Together, we will continue to uncover your passions, develop a roadmap to success, and ensure you have the mindset and tools needed to live out your purpose.

Scan the QR Code below to schedule a 1-on-1 session or to learn more about my speaking engagements and coaching programs.

testimonials

Marquis Thorpe
Chief of Staff, National Security at AWS

QuDerrick Covington's visionary leadership is evident in his ability to conceptualize and implement innovative strategies that propel teams towards their goals, showcasing a keen foresight for the organization's future.

Dr. Roderick Heath
Asst. Vice Chancellor & Dean of Students at Fayetteville State University

As a leader, QuDerrick Covington's vision and strategic thinking have guided teams to unprecedented success, earning him the reputation of an outstanding and influential figure in the industry.

Dr. Tyson Beale
Vice President Student Affairs at Prince George's Community College

QuDerrick Covington's public speaking is unmatched, creating an engaging and inclusive atmosphere at every event. His charisma and seamless execution make him a standout speaker, leaving a lasting positive impact on every attendee.

You can't be competitive without knowing your purpose.

HEAD OVER TO INSTAGRAM & FOLLOW **@QRCOVINGTON** FOR DAILY INSPIRATION + PURPOSE-DRIVEN INSIGHTS!

SECTION EIGHT

Living fully in your purpose.

PROVOKED INTO PURPOSE

FULLY COMMIT TO YOUR PURPOSE, NO MATTER THE COST.

Part 1: Creating a 5-Year Roadmap

Write down your vision for the next 5 years. What are your big goals and dreams?

1. What sacrifices are you willing to make to fully commit to your purpose?
2. How can you stay motivated during challenging times?
3. What does success look like to you when fully living out your purpose?

FULLY COMMIT TO YOUR PURPOSE, NO MATTER THE COST.

Part 1: Creating a 5-Year Roadmap

You will outline a plan for maintaining your commitment to your purposed-driven life, including strategies for overcoming obstacles.

Year 1:

WHY IS THIS IMPORTANT FOR ME?

ACTION STEPS

01

02

03

04

05

06

07

08

09

10

WHAT AM I WILLING TO SACRIFICE

HOW WILL I OVER COME OBSTACLES AND NOISE?

FULLY COMMIT TO YOUR PURPOSE, NO MATTER THE COST.

Part 1: Creating a 5-Year Roadmap

You will outline a plan for maintaining your commitment to your purposed-driven life, including strategies for overcoming obstacles.

Year 2:

WHY IS THIS IMPORTANT FOR ME?

ACTION STEPS

01

02

03

04

05

06

07

08

09

10

WHAT AM I WILLING TO SACRIFICE

HOW WILL I OVER COME OBSTACLES AND NOISE?

FULLY COMMIT TO YOUR PURPOSE, NO MATTER THE COST.

Part 1: Creating a 5-Year Roadmap

You will outline a plan for maintaining your commitment to your purposed-driven life, including strategies for overcoming obstacles.

Year 3:

WHY IS THIS IMPORTANT FOR ME?

ACTION STEPS

01

02

03

04

05

06

07

08

09

10

WHAT AM I WILLING TO SACRIFICE

HOW WILL I OVER COME OBSTACLES AND NOISE?

FULLY COMMIT TO YOUR PURPOSE, NO MATTER THE COST.

Part 1: Creating a 5-Year Roadmap

You will outline a plan for maintaining your commitment to your purposed-driven life, including strategies for overcoming obstacles.

Year 4:

WHY IS THIS IMPORTANT FOR ME?

ACTION STEPS

01

02

03

04

05

06

07

08

09

10

WHAT AM I WILLING TO SACRIFICE

HOW WILL I OVER COME OBSTACLES AND NOISE?

FULLY COMMIT TO YOUR PURPOSE, NO MATTER THE COST.

Part 1: Creating a 5-Year Roadmap

You will outline a plan for maintaining your commitment to your purposed-driven life, including strategies for overcoming obstacles.

Year 5:

WHY IS THIS IMPORTANT FOR ME?

ACTION STEPS

01

02

03

04

05

06

07

08

09

10

WHAT AM I WILLING TO SACRIFICE

HOW WILL I OVER COME OBSTACLES AND NOISE?

FULLY COMMIT TO YOUR PURPOSE, NO MATTER THE COST.

Part 2: Reflection on Sacrifice

Reflect on what pursuing your purpose has cost you.
What have you had to sacrifice to live in alignment with your purpose?
How can you embrace these sacrifices as part of your journey?

FULLY COMMIT TO YOUR PURPOSE, NO MATTER THE COST.

Part 2: Reflection on Sacrifice

Reflect on what pursuing your purpose has cost you.
What have you had to sacrifice to live in alignment with your purpose?
How can you embrace these sacrifices as part of your journey?

TAKE YOUR JOURNEY TO THE NEXT LEVEL

You've made incredible progress through this section, but your journey toward living fully in your purpose is just beginning. If you're ready to dive deeper, work directly with me, Qu'Derrick R. Covington, as your personal purpose coach. Together, we will continue to uncover your passions, develop a roadmap to success, and ensure you have the mindset and tools needed to live out your purpose.

Scan the QR Code below to schedule a 1-on-1 session or to learn more about my speaking engagements and coaching programs.

testimonials

Marquis Thorpe

Chief of Staff, National Security at AWS

QuDerrick Covington's visionary leadership is evident in his ability to conceptualize and implement innovative strategies that propel teams towards their goals, showcasing a keen foresight for the organization's future.

Dr. Roderick Heath

Asst. Vice Chancellor & Dean of Students at Fayetteville State University

As a leader, QuDerrick Covington's vision and strategic thinking have guided teams to unprecedented success, earning him the reputation of an outstanding and influential figure in the industry.

Dr. Tyson Beale

Vice President Student Affairs at Prince George's Community College

QuDerrick Covington's public speaking is unmatched, creating an engaging and inclusive atmosphere at every event. His charisma and seamless execution make him a standout speaker, leaving a lasting positive impact on every attendee.

You can't be competitive without knowing your purpose.

HEAD OVER TO INSTAGRAM & FOLLOW **@QRCOVINGTON** FOR DAILY INSPIRATION + PURPOSE-DRIVEN INSIGHTS!

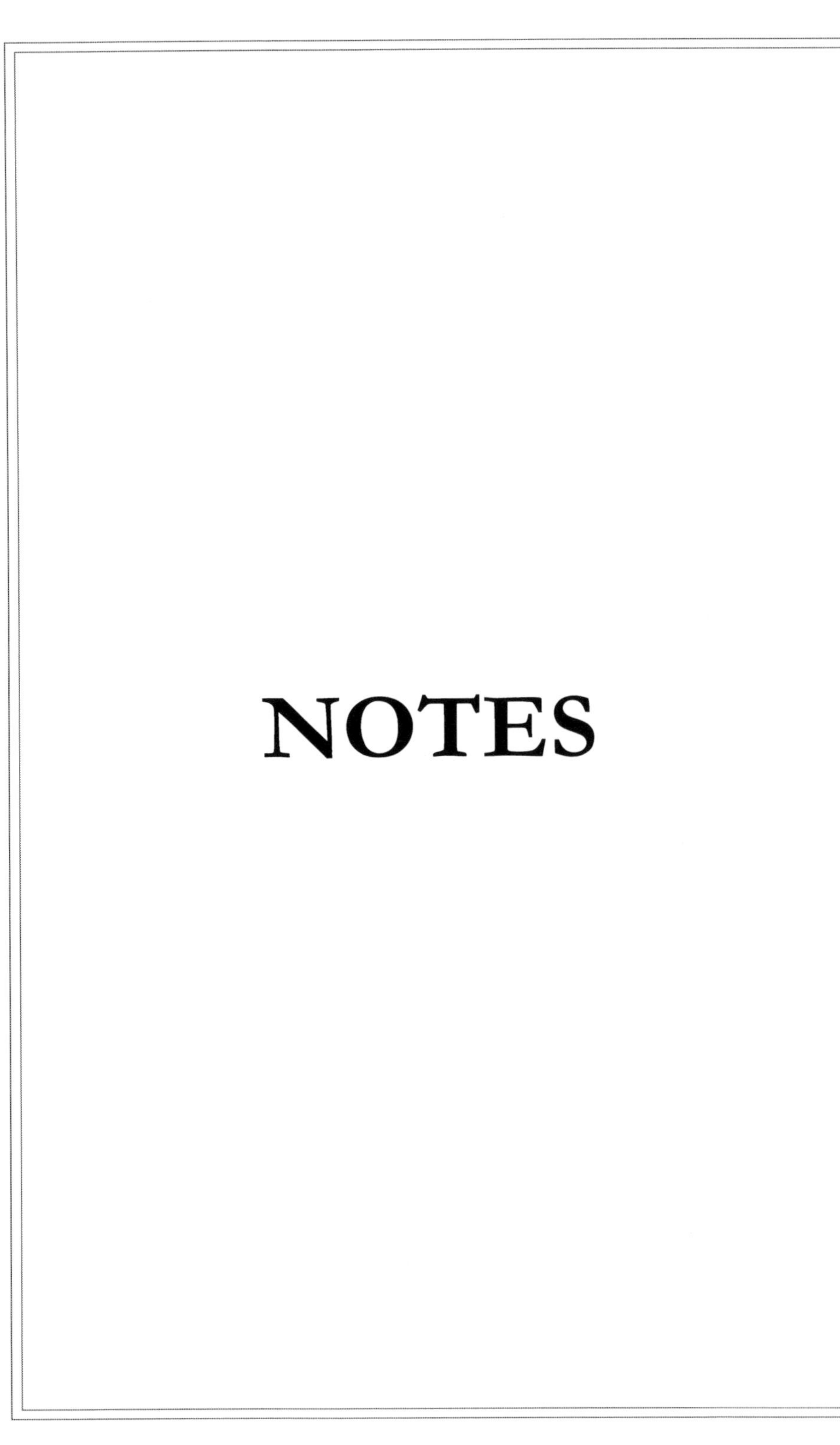

NOTES

You were not
created to simply exist.
You were born to live a life of
meaning, passion, and purpose,
and it starts the moment you decide
to act on what's already within you.

Qu'Derrick R. Covington

Before you go...
I want to hear from you!

Have thoughts or feedback about this section?

Scan the QR code below to provide your input and help improve the Provoked Into Purpose Workbook.

Your feedback is invaluable!

WWW.QRCOVINGTON.COM

Made in the USA
Middletown, DE
21 October 2024